INDIE AUTHORS USER'S GUIDE

A GUIDE TO WRITING & PUBLISHING YOUR OWN BOOKS

CAROL PACK

Artiqua Press

www.artiquapress.com

ARTIQUA PRESS
Westbury, NY 11590
info@artiquapress.com

TRADE PAPERBACK

May 14, 2024

INDIE AUTHORS USER'S GUIDE
A Guide to Writing & Publishing Your Own Books

ISBN: 978-1-970028-15-7

DEDICATION

I dedicate this book to all authors who provide sanctuary to the countless characters who have taken up residency in our brains.

The best way to give those characters their due is to evict them onto the pages of a novel where they can live for the foreseeable future in the hearts and minds of others.

TABLE OF CONTENTS

The Ingredients of All Fiction   1
  Plot, Characters, Setting, Conflict, Point of View,
  Tense, Pacing, Style, Voice, Tone, Genre, Theme

Literary Devices   20
  Allegory, Alliteration, Allusion, Anachronism, Analogy,
  Anaphora, Anthropomorphism, Aphorism, Archetype,
  Epigraph, Euphemism, Foreshadowing, Hyperbole,
  Irony, Juxtaposition, Metaphor, Motif, Onomatopoeia,
  Oxymoron, Paradox, Personification, Simile, Symbolism

A Humorous Look at Writing Rules   25

Writing Your Manuscript   31

Revisions   33
  First Draft, Second Draft, Final Draft

Editing   36
  Developmental/Structural, Substantive/Content,
  Beta Readers, Line Editing, Copyediting, Proofreading

Publishing   41
  Front Matter, Manuscript, Back Matter, ISBN,
  Copyright, LCCN, Metadata

Covering It All   48
  E-book Cover, Print Cover, Trim Size, Page Count, Paper
  Color and Weight, Binding, Barcode, Back-Cover Summary,
  Logline, Elevator Pitch, Book Price, Royalties

Advertising & Marketing   59
  Website, Blogs, Podcasts & Videos, Keywords, SEO,
  Backlinks, Social Media

Printers & Self-Publishing Sites   62

Conclusion   63

Resources   63

Author's Bio   65

PREFACE

You do not need an expensive company to help you publish your books. You're going to end up being your own subcontractor anyway, as far as writing and marketing are concerned, so why pay a ton of money to others to tell you what to do?

When I first decided to self-publish, I had a million and one questions, or at least, it felt that way. I spent countless hours looking up information so I could make informed decisions. I wanted to make my book look as professional as possible in the hope that bookstores would say. *Sure, we'll put your book on our shelves.* That was a pipe dream. For a bookstore to consider my book, I had to discount it by 55 percent and allow returns. The price needed to be high enough to cover printing and handling costs after the discount, yet low enough to entice readers to buy my book, even if they'd never heard of me. That's when I learned a store could purchase copies of your book, only to return them months later with dog-eared pages and soiled covers because they couldn't sell them. After refunding what they paid, I was left with a bunch of unsellable books and a hole in my bank account for unrecoverable printing and handling fees. That business model did not work for me.

Rule number one: Manage your expectations.

I started out buying a single ISBN (International Standard Book Number) for $125.00. Some places offer to give you an ISBN for free, but that makes THEM the publisher. I wanted to create my own imprint and be the publisher. I quickly learned that each version of a book requires its own ISBN, which not only identifies who published it but also whether it is a hardcover, a paperback, an e-book, an audiobook, or any other possibility.

Rule number two: If you plan to write more than one book, you will save a lot by buying ISBNs in bulk.

When I hired a cover designer, he asked me what text I wanted printed on the front and back covers. I labored over the story summary like my life depended on it. That is when I realized that if I wanted to be an indie author, I was ultimately responsible for every word on the inside and outside of my book. Unfortunately, at that point, I had never heard of SEO and didn't know its value.

Rule number three: learn about digitally marketing your books.

Note: In many instances on the following pages, I have used the gender-neutral pronouns they, their, and them to be more inclusive of nonbinary readers. This usage creates a tense problem because they, their, and them are each considered plural, even when I use them to designate singular people. As a copy editor, this disagreement in tense makes me cringe because I think it makes my writing look sloppy. However, I feel I'm now using these words with intention after reading the following posting in the Chicago Manual of Style forum:

"The use of they, their, them, and themselves as pronouns of indefinite gender and indefinite number is well established in speech and writing, even in literary and formal contexts. This gives you the option of using the plural pronouns where you think they sound best, and of using the singular pronouns (such as he, she, he or she, and their inflected forms) where you think they sound best."

Self-publishing taught me a lot. Hopefully, this reference manual will give you some insight so you can spend more time writing and less time looking stuff up.

Please Note: This book is based on US styles and costs, which may not apply to other countries.

INDIE AUTHORS USER'S GUIDE

ABCs OF STORYTELLING

THE INGREDIENTS OF ALL FICTION

PLOT

There are two predominant types of writers: plotters and pantsers. Plotters outline their novels, some loosely, others in great detail. Pantsers write by the seat of their pants. Their novels are more organic. Regardless, if you plan to finish a book, you should have a general idea from the get-go of how the story ends. You want a general destination that your writing compass can guide you toward. A plotter may devise a graph showing specific pages on which various plot turns and resolutions must happen to build momentum evenly. Or they might list the contents of each chapter. A pantser might simply think *Cloe's handbag is stolen in the first chapter, and she recovers it in the last—after following its most unusual journey to strange and distant lands;* just an idea that gives the author some direction.

KEY STORY ELEMENTS

Every story, regardless of genre, should include the following stages:

Stage 1 – Status Quo: Just another day in the life of the protagonist.

Stage 2 – Inciting Incident: Something out of the ordinary happens—a high-stakes problem—that takes the protagonist out of their comfort zone and forces them to make a decision.

Stage 3 – Rising Action: This is where your story arc deepens. It should include a series of additional complications and show how your protagonist responds to each challenge, causing them to change or grow. There should be failures as well as victories.

Stage 4 – Impasse: The protagonist faces an almost insurmountable difficulty.

Stage 5 – Climax: The protagonist must make a difficult choice.

Stage 6 – Resolution: The characters come to terms with what happened, resolve the conflict, and answer questions. The story arc is complete.

Here is a simple example of the stages at work in "The Three Pigs" (the kinder, gentler version):

Status quo: The three pigs set out to build their homes. They each have a different idea of what materials to use and how much effort should go into it.

Inciting incident: A wolf spots them and says he is going to eat them.

Rising action: The pigs hide in their respective homes. The wolf blows down the houses made of straw and wood, but those pigs escape and seek safety in their brother's brick house.

Impasse: The wolf huffs and puffs but can't blow the brick house down.

Climax: The wolf climbs on the roof and sneaks down the chimney. However, the pigs block the fireplace opening with a big pot of boiling water.

Resolution: The wolf is stopped, and the pigs are saved.

Of course, if you're more familiar with the original version of the story, the pigs cook the wolf and eat him for dinner. If that's the ending you prefer to go with, that is your prerogative.

Let's come up with the stages of a different story based on the following prompt.

Amy and her brother Matt inherit a run-down beach cottage.

Status Quo: Amy and her brother Matt have been living together in Amy's apartment ever since Matt lost his job and could no longer pay his rent. They receive a letter saying they've inherited a beach cottage. They visit the rundown cottage, which sits all by itself at the end of the shoreline. The siblings learn the cottage is part of the village's historic district, built by the area's first mayor in 1850.

Inciting Incident: Matt points out several structural issues and says fixing them would be costly because there are strict parameters in place regarding renovation. They decide to sell the cottage. However, its condition and covenants on the property will make selling the house difficult.

Rising Action: Amy convinces Matt that if they fix it up a little, it might be easier to sell. Matt points out that building supplies cost money, and he has none to invest. Amy says she'll contribute money to buy paint and lumber if Matt will do the labor. He agrees. Amy paints the front door and porch while Matt repairs the rotted front steps with new lumber. They each feel optimistic about what they've accomplished.

Impasse: A Realtor points out that they should have fixed the sagging cottage's foundation issues first. Matt looks into it and learns the work will cost thousands of dollars. He's also told he'll have to demolish the new steps he just built to get to that part of the foundation. Matt tells Amy she can keep the money pit they inherited. He needs to find a *real* job. Amy feels like her brother deserted her. Matt feels guilty after hearing his sister's sobs as he walks away from the cottage.

Climax: Matt finds a job, but the company does not need him to start for a month. He returns to the cottage to apologize to Amy and tell her he will continue helping her until he starts work. When he arrives, he finds workers shoring up the foundation. Amy says she took out a loan to repair the foundation and make the cottage livable for herself. A construction worker hauls out a metal box and informs Amy that it was the only thing holding up the foundation in one corner.

Resolution: Amy tries to open the metal box, but it's padlocked. Matt picks up a piece of rubble and smashes the lock. Inside, they find deeds to other parcels of shorefront land. They learn that much of the vacant land surrounding the cottage also belongs to them and realize it's worth a fortune. They sell off a few plots and use that money to restore the cottage.

Coming up with scenarios to fit the key elements of the above prompt took about an hour. You may want to practice on some of the prompts below. There are no right or wrong answers. The results depend on the imagination and interests of each writer. Ten different authors would outline ten different stories depending on each author's experiences.

ADDITIONAL STORY PROMPTS

If you would like to try your hand at developing some prompts, a few are listed below. Have fun with them. Be realistic or outrageous. It's an exercise to help you familiarize yourself with all the stages every protagonist should navigate.

Here are some prompts you can try developing:

a) Two brothers—who haven't spoken to each other since their youngest brother died five years earlier—end up together, locked in the room where their brother committed suicide.

b) Sasha's father is an alcoholic who is physically abusive. One evening, when he attacks Sasha, they grab a frying pan and smash in the side of their father's head.

c) Three fraternity buddies solemnly vow to always come to each other's aid, no matter where life takes them.

d) Madeline has no wish to be betrothed; however, her mother, the duchess, will not rest until her daughter is married.

e) A black hole in space grows dangerously stronger. The inhabitants of the nearest planet fear it will destroy their civilization unless they find a way to stop it.

Status quo:

Inciting element:

Rising Action:

Impasse:

Climax:

Resolution:

CHARACTERS

Characters are as important as the plot. If your characters aren't relatable—if readers don't care about them—people may never finish reading your book. Nor will they recommend it to their friends.

Your *protagonist* should be relatable. People want to be able to depend on the person you have designated as the hero. Heroes should be:

- Driven
- Brave
- Likable

They should not be perfect. Even the nicest people have a character flaw or two. A hero may not always make the correct choice, but at least they will do everything in their power to try to make things right.

They will need a good reason to keep on going, whether it is facing their greatest fear or sacrificing something huge, even if they feel like everything is stacked against their chances of success.

Your *antagonist* needs to be more than "mean or powerful." They often may be:

- Compelled
- Diabolical
- Relentless

However, your villain also needs to have a redeemable feature—something readers can relate to. Perhaps they love animals and have a pet they snuggle with. Or they are a trained assassin who kills adults without a second thought but exhibit a soft spot for children. Maybe they give their scarf or gloves to a homeless person on a wintry night. The antagonist needs to show some vestige of humanity to be believable. Keep in mind, your villain is just as convinced as the hero is that they're fighting for what is "right" (for them).

I have a terrible memory, so I like to create profiles for all of my characters. I base each one on a public figure or celebrity whose description (face and body type) lends itself to the character I'm creating. I usually print out a picture and, on the flip side, note their name, age, and physical characteristics—real and imagined. I'll write in schools and degrees, birth date and astrological sign, hobbies and interests, political and religious beliefs, basically, whatever drives them. Every time I add something to my manuscript, a song a character is humming or a favorite pair of shoes, I note it on their profile. I refer to these pages as my bible. This bible has saved me more than once, and I refer to it often.

SETTING

Settings help establish a mood and a sense of place for readers. They are as important to your story as the plot or the characters and can help establish the tone of your scene. A party isn't just a party. It can be a hoedown, a family free-for-all, or an intimate dinner party. It can be at home, in a bar, or at an elegant restaurant. A business meeting can be in a boardroom full of suits, over a cup of cappuccino in a coffee shop, or on the golf course. Each description conveys a different tone and can be used to change the tension level.

Imagine a meeting between two strangers in a dark forest on a rainy evening with the odor of decomposing flesh hanging in the air. Now imagine it in the middle of a garden party on a sunlit day with soft music in the background and the scent of roses. The setting helps paint the picture and establishes the mood.

- The setting can help you "show—not tell." Describing the atmosphere and involving senses other than sight, like touch and smell, allows the reader to think *gloomy* or *pleasant* without your narrator having to "tell" them. However, only give readers enough description to establish a sense of place. Don't over describe. Use just enough to add subtext to your story. Metaphors can help. Use them to compare something mundane to something more visual: *the dragon spewed flames like the most powerful volcano.* It shouldn't take a lot of words to create a richly textured world.

When writing about the setting, consider:

- Animals
- Architecture
  - Shack vs. Tract house vs. Palace
  - Rented room vs. Apartment vs. Penthouse
  - Cave vs. Tent vs. Trailer
- Building materials
  - Reclaimed barnwood
  - Limestone blocks
  - Steel and glass
- Economy
- Era
  - Stone Age
  - Renaissance
  - Post-modern
- Politics
- Actual location vs. Fictional place
  - Landmarks
  - Population density
  - Ecosystem
- Senses
  - Sight
  - Sound
  - Touch
  - Taste
  - Scent

- Technology
- Time of day / Season / Year
- Topography
  - Village vs. Town vs. City
  - Desert vs. Forest vs. Ocean
  - Mountains vs. Plains vs. Sky
- Weather

An inadequate description will result in what editors call *white room syndrome:* so little setting that your characters could be talking in a white room. However, too much description will slow the pace of your story and could bore your readers. It's all in the balance.

CONFLICT

Every story requires conflict to create narrative tension. Without it, you won't be able to hold your readers' interest. The opposition between what the antagonist wants and what the protagonist is willing to do to prevent it—drives your story forward. Every page, every scene, and every paragraph should embody some of that conflict.

When I hear the word *conflict,* I immediately think of a battle or a war. However, a conflict can simply be a disagreement between two people.

Example no. 1 – Russia wants to grow. There are borders in place. Russia invades Ukraine to expand into that country. That's a conflict. *Don't roll your eyes at me.* My writing about your perceived reaction to the above example is also a conflict.

Example no. 2 – John and Sally agreed to go out together on Saturday night. Sally wants to go roller skating. John would rather go to the movies. That's a conflict.

Example no. 3 – Only *one* of the "most delicious scones ever baked" remains on the kitchen table. Both Dylan and Niall grab for it at the same moment. That's a conflict. Mama settles the imminent fight by saying neither of them can have it and eats it herself. That's another conflict.

Example no. 4 – "You left the cap off the toothpaste again!" A conflict.

Example no. 5 – Granny finishes watering her prized tulips. She can imagine a first-place ribbon in her hand at the country fair. She stands and brushes the dirt off her knees as her beloved 3-year-old granddaughter rushes to her, hugging her legs. After a quick kiss, the little girl says, "Pretty," and plucks the most beautiful tulip, running off with it. *Conflict.*

However, for the sake of your novel, let's focus on the main conflict that moves your plot forward. As your hero works to succeed, each new obstacle should be more challenging to overcome than the previous ones. So, you may want to preplan ways to increase the conflict in each succeeding scene.

There are various ways to do that. Make your hero do something they would never choose to do. It can be a moral dilemma or facing something they fear. Think of Indiana Jones and how much he hated snakes. Perhaps your hero must hurt or lose someone or something they love. Or they might make a choice that turns out to be the wrong one. Perhaps that choice was based on a misunderstanding. Maybe it turns everyone against them. The hero's last obstacle should be something they feel doomed to fail at.

Keep in mind that inserting additional (or different) conflicts in a later draft of your story may require foreshadowing. It will make more sense when your hero moans while being attacked by arachnids if an earlier scene talks about how they wandered into a nest of spiders as a child and was traumatized by multiple spider bites.

POINT OF VIEW

Point of view, or POV, refers to who is describing the action in a story. Who is the narrator?

First-person POV: The narrator and the protagonist are the same person. The story is told from the protagonist's perspective. "I was six when I first witnessed a murder." First-person narrators can only talk about the experiences they have personally had but not what anyone else is thinking.

Second-person POV: The story is told from the reader's perspective. "You were six when you first witnessed a murder." This POV is rarely used when writing fiction but is popular for blogs, videos, and self-help books, i.e., "And when you do this stretch, you'll feel it in your hamstrings."

Third-person POV: An external narrator tells the story. "Henry was six when he first witnessed a murder." This is the most used POV for fiction writers. All my books, to date, have been written in third-person omniscient.

One of the problems of third-person omniscient is that it allows the narrator to know what each person is thinking, but all those different points of view can confuse readers in a scene. Jumping from one character's POV to another is commonly called "head hopping" and is a common problem, especially for new authors. To avoid it, don't switch POV mid-scene. Start a new scene or paragraph to change the POV.

If it is impractical to start a new scene, try describing the intruding character's actions rather than their thoughts. For example, if the scene is all about John's feelings as he's proposing to Annie, but suddenly, we are inside Annie's head hearing how she should be taking a selfie of her beautifully plated dinner, the switch in POV might take the reader out of the moment. To rectify the problem, you could always describe Annie's actions rather than her thoughts.

> *John stammered as he told Annie about his feelings for her and paused to take out a ring box. Annie stared at her dinner plate before grabbing her cell phone and zeroing in on her entree. Before she could snap a photo, John dropped to one knee, opening a tiny blue box that he held out to her. Annie swung the viewfinder from her dinner plate to a diamond ring and gasped.*

TENSE

Most books are written in present or past tense, with past tense the more popular choice. It is what most adult readers are used to.

> Past tense: *She walked across the floor and opened the door. Everything happened so quickly, she didn't see the blade come down.*

However, some younger writers are now writing in the present tense, and their readers are becoming used to it.

> Present tense: *She walks across the floor and opens the door. Everything happens quickly. She doesn't see the blade coming down.*

Present-tense stories in first person are probably the most intimate—as if the reader and the protagonist are the same person.

> Present tense/first person: *I walk across the floor and open the door.*

Everything is a blur. I hear a whisper of sound—

Present tense/first person limits your writing because, unless the protagonist can read minds, he won't know what anyone else is thinking or feeling. You can describe the actions that others take but not their thoughts. You can *show*, but you can't *tell*.

> *I drop the gun.*
> *Shayna's eyes widen as she stares at me. Tears stream down her face as she presses her hands against her chest.*
> *I watch in horror as her fingers and shirt grow red with blood.*

PACING

Pacing refers to the ebb and flow of your novel. Think of a fast-paced thriller versus a slower-paced romance. A faster pace can create excitement and suspense; a slower pace allows introspection and emotional depth.

Every story should have varied pacing. Use it to prevent overwhelming your readers. After a particularly tense scene, ease the pace to allow readers to breathe. Think of it like a symphony. Music uses various movements and tempos to express a series of emotions. In a similar way, manuscripts should have varied pacing with high and low action to keep readers engaged and entertained. However, the pacing needs to make sense.

You don't want an entire book to unfold at breakneck speed. That would be exhausting. Neither would you want it to plod lazily (and boringly) toward a climax. Consider each scene and how using pace can help it reach its full potential.

Increase pacing with:

- Action
- Active voice
- Conflict
- Dialogue, especially quick, snappy repartee
- Frequent scene changes
- Short, choppy sentences
- Shorter chapters

Decrease pacing with:

- Detailed description
- Languid narration
- Internal dialogue *(what a character is thinking)*
- Longer chapters, scenes, and sentences
- Serene language

STYLE

Merriam-Webster's Collegiate Dictionary defines style as a distinctive manner of expression. For a writer, style means the vocabulary you choose, the length of your sentences, and how you structure those sentences. Do you write compound-complex sentences with lush imagery and imaginative descriptions? Or do you prefer simple sentences punctuated with humor and wit? The ways you choose to put words together define your overall style.

VOICE

Voice describes how an author narrates the story through the eyes of a character, usually the protagonist. A character's individual behavior, thoughts, mannerisms, and dialogue form a voice that is uniquely its own. Say you have two evenly matched detectives from different geographic locations. The city detective may be a no-nonsense, fast talker with slick jargon. A rural counterpart may take life more slowly and speak in longer sentences using a lot of folksy metaphors. Those are their distinct voices.

In addition to the individual characters, authors also have a "voice." It is evident in the rhythm and structure of a story and how it ebbs and flows and develops. It is the writer's fingerprint, distinguishing them from everyone else, and includes:

- Rhythm or cadence of the words
- Choice of words and their formality or informality
- Punctuation and how words are grouped together

TONE

Writers can fine-tune their work depending on the tone they employ.

Formal tone uses the detachment of third person. It is polite—proper—and respectful. It is not folksy. It does not use contractions. It is impersonal, businesslike, and logical. I would describe it as *writing at arm's length.*

Informal tone feels much more familiar. It's like a personal conversation. It's easy and unpretentious. The writing is looser and may include contractions. It often uses emotion to draw people in.

However, tone can say so much more. Your words can sound funny, condescending, facetious, serious, or threatening. Tone can shed light on what you are really thinking, even when your words do not.

Tone can be described in many ways, including:

- Brash
- Happy
- Intense
- Ironic
- Jaded
- Judgmental
- Light
- Playful
- Rushed
- Sarcastic
- Scary
- Sexy
- Temperamental

Think of it as the overall attitude of the subject matter. The opposite side of the coin is *mood*. While tone conveys the writer's attitude, mood is the feeling readers get when reading your story.

GENRE

Genre defines the subject matter of your book or the category your work falls under.

Following are some popular genres with a brief listing of a few of their elements:

Action/Adventure – hero's journey; a quest; fast-paced storyline; dangerous situations; tension; satisfying climax

Detective/Crime – perfect crime; wrongly accused suspect; tenacious detective; unexpected ending

Fantasy – magic; often inspired by mythology or folklore; imaginary setting; established hierarchy or system of power

Gothic – atmospheric setting; elements of suspense; the supernatural

Historical – details of a distinct era; real and fictional characters and places; includes the social conditions and manners of the time period

Mystery – crime or puzzle; detective; overt clues; hidden evidence; red herrings; unexpected villain; satisfying climax

Psychological/Suspense – fear and anxiety driven; unpredictable; believable characters; dysfunctional relationships; unsettling action; emotional; builds slowly

Roman à Clef – fictional characters and places are used to tell the stories of real people, blurring the lines between fact and fiction; satire; allegory

Romance – attraction and conflict; denial; forced togetherness; physical intimacy; misunderstanding; ensuing misery forces the couple to resolve problems

Science Fiction – imaginative, often futuristic storylines; could include space aliens, mythic superheroes, or a zombie apocalypse; uses plausible science or technology to enhance believability; world-building

Thriller – hero; villain; increasing stakes; plot twists; red herrings; false endings; cliffhangers; (see also action/adventure)

Western – often set in a desolate landscape; lawlessness; cowboys; saloons; shootouts; gunslingers; sheriff/ranger/posse

Young Adult – geared toward teenagers and high schoolers, YA is defined more by the age of its protagonists (12–18) and can cover a gamut of genres and themes from young love to historical fiction to dystopian sci-fi thriller

AUDIENCE AGE GROUPS

Children 0 – 2	Simple books, few words
Children 3 – 5	Picture books
Children 6 – 8	Early readers
Middle School 9 – 12	Preteen chapter books
Young Adult 13 – 17	Teen chapter books
New Adult 18 – 25	Chapter books with early adult themes
Adult	All other

THEME

Theme refers to the core message of your story, the overall idea that moves it forward. And once you read the following list, you'll say, "Oh. Yeah. I knew that."

Betrayal – the loss of trust
Circle of life – what goes around comes around
Coming of age – memorable experiences growing up
Death – dying, immortality
Faith vs. Doubt – believing isn't easy
Family – the intricate ties and breaks among family members
Good vs. Evil – the eternal conflict
Hubris – Excessive pride or arrogance
Identity – who am I?
Justice – righting a perceived wrong
Loneliness – grappling with isolation—even in a crowded room
Love – conflicts posed by discovering it, pursuing it, ending it
Man vs. Himself – fighting against long-held beliefs
Man vs. Man – war
Man vs. Nature – surviving what is beyond our control
Man vs. Society – going against *the system*; fighting corruption

Perseverance – persistence to achieve something despite difficulty
Redemption – saving or being saved from sin
Revenge – getting back at someone for a perceived wrong
Sacrifice – giving up everything for someone or something

LITERARY DEVICES

ALLEGORY – a narrative or visual representation in which a character, place, or event can be interpreted to represent a meaning with moral or political significance. Parables, myths, and fables are considered allegories.

> The story of the apple falling onto Isaac Newton's head exemplifies the idea of gravity by depicting a simple way in which it may have been discovered.

ALLITERATION – the repetition of a letter or sound at the beginning of nearby words.

- **S**he **s**ells **s**eashells at the **s**eashore
- **W**etzel's **Pretzels**
- "**W**hisper **w**ords of **w**isdom, let it be." —The Beatles, *Let It Be*

ALLUSION – calling something to mind without specifically mentioning it.

> Chocolate is my *kryptonite*. (Kryptonite alludes to weakness).

ANACHRONISM – something that is out of sync with the time period it appears in; a chronological inconsistency.

- A telephone pictured in a cave drawing
- A microwave oven in Victorian England
- High-top sneakers on a Revolutionary War soldier

ANALOGY – a comparison between two things that is then explained.

> "Life is like a box of chocolate. You never know what you're gonna get." —*Forrest Gump*

ANAPHORA – the repetition of phrases or words to add effect.

- **Give me** liberty, or **give me** death
- **I wish I** may, **I wish I** might
- **It was the** best **of times**, **it was the** worst **of times**

ANTHROPOMORPHISM – gives human-like characteristics or behaviors to animals or inanimate objects.

- Disney Characters
- Dancing boxes of popcorn and snacks in a movie theater promo
- Team Mascots

APHORISM – a short, memorable statement that becomes a popular saying.

- "Don't judge a book by its cover." —George Eliot
- "A penny saved is a penny earned." —Benjamin Franklin
- "May the force be with you." — Jedi Master Obi-Wan Kenobi

ARCHETYPE – a universal symbol that brings familiarity and context to a character or story.

- The "Hero" protagonist
- The "Villain" antagonist
- The "Rags to Riches" story arc

EPIGRAPH – a short quotation or saying at the beginning of a book or chapter intended to suggest its theme.

> "If music be the food of love, play on." —William Shakespeare, *Twelfth Night,* centered on an otherwise blank page before the first entry in a book of poetry

EUPHEMISM – a milder description that replaces a harsh word.

- "Darn" instead of "damn"
- "Heck" instead of "hell"
- "Curvy" instead of "fat"

FORESHADOWING – a tease or advance hint of what's to come.

- The sky darkening before a storm in a thriller
- "I see dead people. … They don't know they're dead." —*The Sixth Sense*
- A French soldier telling King Arthur "Already got one" when Arthur speaks about his quest for the grail at the beginning of *Monty Python and the Holy Grail*

HYPERBOLE – using exaggeration to emphasize dramatic effect.

- My new shoes are **killing** me.
- I gained a **ton** of weight.
- They're **drowning** in money.

IRONY – contrasts expectation and reality.

- A firehouse burns down
- A police officer is robbed
- A librarian yells, "QUIET!"

JUXTAPOSITION – placing two contrasting concepts together to highlight their differences.

- "All is fair in **love** and **war**." —John Lyly
- "It was the **best** of times, it was the **worst** of times." —Charles Dickens, *A Tale of Two Cities*
- The couple had a **love-hate** relationship.

METAPHOR – using a word or phrase denoting one thing to suggest a likeness to something else.

- I'm such a **couch potato**.
- He's like a **dog with a bone**.
- She's a **ticking bomb**.

MOTIF – a recurring thematic symbol; a simple detail repeated for a larger symbolic meaning.

- The rose in *Beauty and the Beast*
- Wicked stepmothers in fairy tales
- Tumbleweeds in westerns

ONOMATOPOEIA – a word that phonetically imitates the sound it describes.

- Oink
- Vroom
- Achoo

OXYMORON – adjacent words that are contradictory.

- Jumbo shrimp
- Old news
- Crash landing

PARADOX – seemingly contradictory statements that could be true.

- You have to spend money to make money.
- Deep down, you're really shallow.
- This is the beginning of the end.

PERSONIFICATION – giving objects human characteristics or emotions.

- The flowers **danced** in the wind.
- The last slice of chocolate cake **called** my name.
- The trees **whispered** in the breeze.

SIMILE – compares two different things using the word "like."

- She had skin like peach fuzz.
- "Oh my love is like a red, red, rose." —Robert Burns
- Their home is like a prison.

SYMBOLISM – images that represent something beyond their literal meaning.

- Pumpkins – Halloween
- Doves – Peace
- Phoenix – Rebirth

A HUMOROUS LOOK AT WRITING RULES BY OTHERS

The website www.plainlanguage.gov has a resource called "How to Write Good." I love the advice and the way it is presented, which highlights what *not* to do. I hesitated to print it here without permission, fearing copyright infringement. However, the site clearly states, "You may use any of the content on this site without explicit permission. As a federal website, the content is in the public domain."

And so, it follows (verbatim):

HOW TO WRITE GOOD

1.   Avoid Alliteration. Always.

2.   Prepositions are not words to end sentences with.

3.   Avoid cliches like the plague. (They're old hat.)

4.   Employ the vernacular.

5.   Eschew ampersands & abbreviations, etc.

6.   Parenthetical remarks (however relevant) are unnecessary.

7.   It is wrong to ever split an infinitive.

8.   Contractions aren't necessary.

9.   Foreign words and phrases are not apropos.

10.   One should never generalize.

11.   Eliminate quotations. As Ralph Waldo Emerson once said, "I hate quotations. Tell me what you know."

12.   Comparisons are as bad as cliches.

13.   Don't be redundant; don't use more words than necessary; it's highly superfluous.

14.   Profanity sucks.

15.   Be more or less specific.

16.   Understatement is always best.

17.   Exaggeration is a billion times worse than understatement.

18.   One word sentences? Eliminate.

19.   Analogies in writing are like feathers on a snake.

20.   The passive voice is to be avoided.

21.   Go around the barn at high noon to avoid colloquialisms.

22.   Even if a mixed metaphor sings, it should be derailed.

23.   Who needs rhetorical questions?

* * *

24.   Parenthetical words however must be enclosed in commas.

25.   It behooves you to avoid archaic expressions.

26.   Avoid archaeic spellings too.

27.   Don't repeat yourself, or say again what you have said before.

28.   Don't use commas, that, are not, necessary.

29.   Do not use hyperbole; not one in a million can do it effectively.

30. Never use a big word when a diminutive alternative would suffice.

31. Subject and verb always has to agree.

32. Placing a comma between subject and predicate, is not correct.

33. Use youre spell chekker to avoid mispeling and to catch typograhpical errers.

34. Don't repeat yourself, or say again what you have said before.

35. Use the apostrophe in it's proper place and omit it when its not needed.

36. Don't never use no double negatives.

37. Poofread carefully to see if you any words out.

38. Hopefully, you will use words correctly, irregardless of how others use them.

39. Eschew obfuscation.

40. No sentence fragments.

41. Don't indulge in sesquipedalian lexicological constructions.

42. A writer must not shift your point of view.

43. Don't overuse exclamation marks!!

44. Place pronouns as close as possible, especially in long sentences, as of 10 or more words, to their antecedents.

45. Writing carefully, dangling participles must be avoided.

46. If any word is improper at the end of a sentence, a linking verb is.

47.   Avoid trendy locutions that sound flaky.

48.   Everyone should be careful to use a singular pronoun with singular nouns in their writing.

49.   Always pick on the correct idiom.

50.   The adverb always follows the verb.

51.   Take the bull by the hand and avoid mixing metaphors.

52.   If you reread your work, you can find on rereading a great deal of repetition can be by rereading and editing.

53.   And always be sure to finish what

As noted on www.plainlanguage.gov, Frank L. Visco wrote the first twenty-three entries for *Writers Digest* (June 1986), and William Safire based rules twenty-four through fifty-three on *William Safire's Rules for Writers*.

INDIE AUTHORS USER'S GUIDE

WRITING & EDITING YOUR MANUSCRIPT

WRITING YOUR MANUSCRIPT

If all you do is talk about writing a book—but never actually complete a manuscript—you're nothing more than a *wannabe*. However, if you're serious about a career as a writer, here are some tips to take with you on your journey.

1. Put pen to paper. Or fingers to keyboard. Or vocal cords to recording device. Use whatever method works for you. Thinking about writing won't make you a novelist. Doing it will.

2. Come up with a hook. This will go on your first page and should engage readers while foreshadowing the story ahead.

3. Do not go back to edit your work until you have completed the first draft. If you go back too soon, you may become enmeshed in an endless loop of second-guessing your words and never complete the manuscript. It's called a first draft for a reason. Keep moving forward. You'll have plenty of time to revise and edit once you have set down the skeleton of your story.

4. Commit to a regular writing schedule. Select a time each day that you can devote to writing. Maybe it's in the evening when your home is quiet. Maybe it's on your lunch hour while at work. Maybe it's weekend afternoons. It's better to work every day. However, as long as you continue to move forward—even if you only have a day or two a week to write—you'll see progress.

5. Try to write a minimum number of words during each work session. Most manuscripts are usually written on letter-size paper with one-inch margins in 12-point Times New Roman font with double-spaced lines. Doing so results in approximately 250 words per page. How many pages you can write, depends on how much time you can invest in each session. I try to write 1,000 words in a 4-hour session, which works out to about a page an hour. At that rate, I could theoretically write an 80,000-word book in less than three months—if I

write every day. Even if someone could only devote half that time to writing, they could finish a manuscript in six months.

6. The goal of your first draft is to tell a complete story with a beginning, a middle, and an end.

7. Some of your writing time may be devoted to research. It may not add pages to your manuscript but that's okay because research is an important part of the process.

8. Once you complete your first draft, let it sit for a while before you go back to rewrite it.

9. When you reread your first draft, there will probably be a thousand things you want to change. This may be a good time to decide whether you would benefit from a structural or developmental edit of your manuscript.

10. If you forego a structural/developmental edit, take the time to ensure your manuscript includes all the stages listed in the key plot elements at the beginning of this guide.

WHAT TO AVOID

Information dumps – also known as backstory—can bog down the flow of a story, especially at the beginning of the book. Think of it like an artichoke. Eating one leaf at a time is better than trying to stuff the whole thing down your throat.

Formatting – can cause more problems than it's worth. At this early stage, your manuscript should be no-frills. Don't try to get fancy by using different fonts and sizes or adding glyphs. Doing that can turn into a nightmare when you try to publish your book. I wrote a YA series in which a group of characters all had symbols instead of names. When I tried to convert the text for an e-book, I ended up with a lot of empty little boxes instead of the various symbols I had chosen, and they played havoc with the spacing. Don't get overly *decorative* when writing your first draft, especially if you plan to publish it yourself.

REVISIONS

REVIEWING YOUR FIRST DRAFT

Take a tip from some copy editors—when you review your first draft for the first time, use colored pens to mark areas that need more work. However, try not to stop to rewrite. Continue reading. You don't want to take yourself out of the flow of the story.

This first pass is to identify what is incorrect, incomplete, or just not working. *That* is best served by reading your novel like a reader would. Mark the plot holes; make an arrow next to scenes, paragraphs, and chapters that need to be moved earlier or later in your timeline; place a check mark next to anything that bothers you. Mark the entire manuscript. But don't make the actual changes until after you've read it completely.

SECOND DRAFT

1. Fill in the blanks. Look for plot holes, or areas that need more description or dialogue, and write what is necessary.
2. If scenes seem out of order, move them. This is a good time to construct a style sheet and a timeline.
3. Make sure all your main characters are relatable. You want readers to care about what happens to them. Even the villain needs to have at least one good quality. However, your hero should not be perfect. Human beings are flawed, and your protagonist should be as well.
4. Too many characters can be confusing to readers. Make sure their names and personalities are distinct. If you have a lot of characters, you may want to combine minor ones or completely remove them if they don't move the plot forward.

5. Rewrite anything that sounds stilted. Change passive sentences into active ones unless doing so changes the intent of the sentence or scene. If you notice the same word or words popping up in close proximity repeatedly, you may need to find synonyms or rewrite those sentences.

6. If you are writing a novel, now is a good time to make sure your subplot supports your main plot and that all the strings of your subplots are neatly tied up.

7. You've probably heard the term "kill your darlings." It is advice credited to William Faulkner, re-stated by Stephen King, and possibly originated by Arthur Quiller-Couch who advised people to "Murder your darlings" in a 1914 essay. It means when you hit a passage you love that does nothing to move the plot forward, get rid of it. It may seem precious to you, but if it doesn't serve the story, it's working against you.

8. Does the middle of your plot sag? Check your rising action. Each successive roadblock to the hero's success should be more challenging to get past than the ones before it. You may need to make some additions or subtractions or to do some rearranging. This is no place to get lazy. You want your book to be the best it can be.

9. After you have finished your second draft, you may want to hire a copy editor. They will help catch anything you missed and suggest ways to improve the flow of your prose.

10. This might also be a good time to ask a few people—who you know will be brutally honest with you—to *beta read* your book. Explain that you want their general observations about plot holes, weak characters, setting, pacing, and inconsistencies. Keep an open mind and give serious thought to what they tell you. Some of it may be a personal preference on their part. But if two or three people point out the same problem, you have some work ahead of you.

FINAL DRAFT

1. Be aware that the final draft of your manuscript may not be your third draft; it could be your fifth, tenth, or twentieth rewrite. There is no set number. It takes how many times it takes until the story is right.

2. Incorporate changes based on your copy editor's and beta readers' feedback.

3. Be aware that you risk adding potential misspellings, grammatical problems, and punctuation mistakes every time you change a manuscript. You may correct a word and mistakenly erase the period that comes after it. Or perhaps you changed a phrase, and now there is a double word. Or a missing word. That said, after writing your final draft, you may want to hire a proofreader.

You want the final draft of your book to be a polished manuscript worthy of publication.

EDITING

Approximately 60 percent of indie authors have their books professionally edited, according to a survey by Written Word Media. Submitting your manuscript for several different levels of editing may be cost prohibitive. However, hiring a good developmental editor could be a wise investment if you are just starting out. The results may open your eyes to any inherent weaknesses in your writing and could help you not only correct problems in your current books but avoid them in future books. Following is a brief review of the different types of editing.

STRUCTURAL/DEVELOPMENTAL EDITING

Developmental editing is done during the early stages of a manuscript. It looks at the manuscript as a whole and points out essential parts of the structure that are missing. Developmental editors often help with dialogue, characters, settings, subplots, readability, and voice and will call your attention to any deficiencies.

SUBSTANTIVE/CONTENT EDITING

If you're further along in the writer's journey and your manuscript is complete, you may want to hire a content editor. Like a developmental editor, a content editor looks at the big picture. They can point out problems with story arcs, plot development, conflict, and points of view.

BETA READERS

I like to have beta readers look at completed versions of my books and tell me what they like and don't like about them. They can point out where they think a story needs improvement—like a subplot that has no resolution or a protagonist that should be relatable but is not. Ask them to let you know if they think there are any glaring problems or omissions. Just remember, beta readers are usually *civilians*—unpaid family and friends—so they're giving you feedback from a reader's point of view as opposed to a professional one.

Note: There are beta readers for hire who charge a fee for their services. However, I have never used one and have no opinion about their value.

LINE EDITING

A good line editor will dive into the style and readability of your manuscript line by line and help with pacing. Line editors will help you polish the language you use to tell a story and tighten your sentence structure.

COPY EDITING

Copy editors ensure your words are grammatical and your punctuation is correct. They will look for typos and misspellings. Copy editors often combine the talents of line editors and proofreaders, pointing out where your wording can be made stronger and easier to understand while looking for technical errors in your writing.

PROOFREADING

Proofreaders form your last line of defense. After you have made all your corrections and changes and you've written your final word, it is often practical to employ a proofreader to fix any mistakes left behind from the editing process. Every time you change your manuscript, you set yourself up for double words, misspelled words, punctuation errors, and omissions. Proofreading should be the last stage of the writing process so that once you go over it, you can use the "clean" copy of your manuscript that your proofreader returns to you as a basis for your e-book or the text block in your print book.

When you're traditionally published, any combination of these different types of editors might work on your manuscript, and your publisher would foot the bill. However, if you take the indie route, having your book edited rests squarely on your shoulders.

Do you need all these editors? Probably not. A good developmental editor will place you on the right path if need be. And if your beta readers are family and friends—and are free—why not use them? A copy editor, toward the end of your journey, should ensure your prose flows cleanly. At the very least, have a proofreader go over your finished manuscript. Readers are much more forgiving if a missing punctuation mark or misspelled word doesn't take them *out of the moment.*

INDIE AUTHORS USER'S GUIDE

PUBLISHING YOUR MANUSCRIPT

PUBLISHING

Before publishing your book, you should have all the necessary elements in place. Think of it like a recipe; you can't bake a tasty cake if one of the ingredients is missing. We have already gone over writing and editing. From this point on, consider your *completed manuscript* the main ingredient of your book. However, keep in mind it is not the only ingredient.

The following list outlines what else you might need to publish your book.

FRONT MATTER

Although your story begins with chapter one, or in some cases, a prologue, the interior of your book—or text block—begins with front matter. These are all the pages readers see before the actual story unfolds.

Most writers in the US are familiar with books beginning on a right-hand page. In the publishing industry, the right-hand page is referred to as *recto*. I like to think the "r" in recto stands for *right*. Considering page one is recto, it should be easy to remember all odd-numbered pages are recto pages. Left-hand pages are called *verso* (back page) and will always be the even-numbered pages.

Do you need to know this? Maybe not. It may come up once in a blue moon, or you could always drop it into a conversation to impress your friends. E-books "flow" digitally, so there is no recto and verso. However, page location matters in print, and certain pages must be on a specific side. It's essential for indie publishers to keep their right and left-hand pages straight if they plan to sell print books.

The half-title page, title page, dedication page, and, in many instances, chapter headers are printed on recto or right-hand pages. The copyright page is almost always a verso page usually found on the back of the title page.

Here's a checklist of front matter:

☑   The first page inside a print book is usually blank on both front and back (not applicable to e-books)

☑   Half-Title Page – It includes the title and—more often than not—the author's name (this page is not strictly necessary)

☑   Title Page – Title, subtitle, author's name, publisher's name

☑   Copyright Page – Usually found on the back of the title page, it includes technical information about the book: a disclaimer, permissions notice, copyright notice, rights reserved notice, publisher's name and address, publication date, ISBN, LCCN, credits to editors, artists, photographers, etc., and the printing edition

☑   Dedication (optional)

☑   Table of Contents (if necessary)

If you choose to insert page numbers on front matter, they are usually lower-case Roman numerals (i, ii, iii, etc.) rather than digits.

MANUSCRIPT

The manuscript of your novel makes up the bulk of your text block and immediately follows the front matter on the first available recto page.

The page numbers in this part of your book are identified by digits (1, 2, 3, etc.).

BACK MATTER

Following is a list of the pages that readers might find in the back matter of a book.

☑ A call to action asking readers to review the book, or recommend it

☑ Excerpt of the first chapter of the next novel in a series

☑ Acknowledgments to all the people who helped you with the writing and publication of your book

☑ Other Books you have written (this is sometimes included in the front matter)

☑ About the Author (optional short biography)

INDIE AUTHORS
USER'S GUIDE

A GUIDE TO WRITING & PUBLISHING
YOUR OWN BOOKS

CAROL PACK

Artiqua Press

www.artiquapress.com

Title Page

INDIE AUTHORS
USER'S GUIDE

Half-Title Page

ARTIQUA PRESS
Westbury, NY 11590
info@artiquapress.com

E-BOOK

April 30, 2024

INDIE NOVELISTS' USER'S MANUAL
A Guide to Writing & Publishing Your Own Book

Copyright © 2024 Carol Pack for CAP Proofreading & Editing

All rights reserved.

ISBN: 978-1-970028-13-3

"How to Write Good" from the website: www.plainlanguage.gov clearly states: "You may use any of the content on this site without explicit permission. As a federal website, the content is in the public domain."

Copyright Page

Dedication

This book is dedicated to all authors who are providing sanctuary for countless characters who have taken up residency in our brains.

The best way to give them their due is to evict them onto the pages of a novel where they can live forever.

Dedication Page

ISBN

ISBN—or International Standard Book Number—identifies a book's publisher and its title, edition, and format. You will usually find them on the copyright page and embedded in the barcode. In the US, you can purchase ISBNs online from Bowker. If you plan to write more than one book or publish in more than one format, consider buying ISBNs in bulk.

> One ISBN.........$125.00 (a hefty price to pay)
> Ten ISBNs..........$295.00 in total (or 29.50 each)
> 100 ISBNs.........$575.00 in total (or 5.75 each)
> 1,000 ISBNs.........$1,500.00 in total (or 1.50 each)

You can see how buying multiples will save you money. If you plan on publishing both a paperback and a hardcover, they will each need their own ISBN, so you may as well spend a little extra now for a better deal in the long run.

COPYRIGHT

As soon as your original completed manuscript is written, typed, or printed, it is protected by copyright. However, there are further steps you can take to protect your manuscript, like applying to register it with the US Copyright Office.

https://stream-media.loc.gov/copyright/standard.mp4

There is a fee to register, and you will have to send in a copy of your book, but this will give you added protection in the courts if someone infringes on your copyright.

Some things cannot be copyrighted (although they may be protected as trademarks):

- Names
- Titles
- Slogans
- Short phrases
- Ideas
- Facts
- Concepts
- Procedures
- Discoveries
- Lists of ingredients
- Creations that are not fixed in a tangible form

You may have seen something called the "poor man's copyright," which is the process of mailing your work to yourself and leaving the postmarked envelope sealed. According to the US Copyright Office, this is not a substitution for registration, and it says, "There is no provision in the copyright law regarding any such type of protection."

LCCN

An LCCN is another number you may want to have at your fingertips. LCCN is shorthand for Library of Congress Control Number. It is a unique identifying number for your book that is included on the copyright page once it is published. Unlike an ISBN, you will need only one LCCN to identify all formats and editions of a specific title.

Create a PrePub Book Link to apply for an LCCN using this link: https://locexternal.servicenowservices.com/auth

Before you start, you will need to know:

- Audience (are readers middle school, new adult, trade, etc.)
- Age (for children's books)
- Grade levels (for children's books)
- Number of pages
- Publication date
- Language
- Contributors (authors, illustrators, etc.)
- Title
- Publisher's name
- City of publication
- Edition
- Volume information
- 13-digit ISBN

METADATA

Metadata is the information you use to describe your book, like:

- Title
- Author
- ISBN
- Date published
- Price
- Description

COVERING IT ALL

They say *you can't judge a book by its cover,* but many readers do, and if you want them to read your book, it needs to have an appealing cover. Most people in the publishing industry will tell you—if you're going to splurge on anything—invest in a professionally designed cover.

Before you continue, you should have the necessary elements and information on hand. E-books are relatively simple because you only need a front cover. Print books are trickier because you need exact book dimensions, weight and color of the paper used, your total number of pages, an ISBN, a bar code, the type of binding you want, and anything you want printed on the spine besides the title and your name (e.g., an imprint logo). You will also need a back cover summary of your content, an optional one or two-sentence bio of yourself as the author, an optional headshot of yourself, and, if you created your own imprint, your publishing imprint name, logo and web address.

It wouldn't hurt to have a logline prepared: a single sentence that summarizes the central conflict of your plot and hooks the reader. You may want to include it on either the front or back cover, and you can always use it for your 'elevator pitch.'

E-BOOK COVER

Your cover should be easy to see and read in thumbnail size; however, that doesn't mean you should design a tiny cover. KDP recommends using an image size that's 1,600 pixels wide by 2,560 pixels high so that it displays well on high-definition screens. The ideal height-to-width ratio is 1.6:1. That means for every 1,000 pixels in width, you'll want to have 1,600 pixels in height. I recommend using a professional cover designer, but for those of you intent on creating your own cover, remember to use an RBG color profile and 300 dpi for your original e-book artwork. You can always make a duplicate image and reduce the dpi later if the original file size is too large for your purposes.

PRINT BOOK COVER

Print books come in all shapes and sizes. The type of paper used can vary, and so can the bindings. There are also different considerations for hardcover vs. paperback. The cover design depends on the dimensions of your book, so you will need to decide on a trim size before you have it designed. And unlike e-books, print covers require a CMYK color profile with 300 dpi.

TRIM SIZE

There are standard book sizes that readers associate with certain genres. A few of the sizes recommended by IngramSpark follow:

- Thrillers & Mysteries: 5.25" x 8"
- YA General Fiction: 5" x 7"
- YA Dystopian, Fantasy, and Sci-Fi: 5.5" x 8.5"
- General Fiction: 6" x 9"
- General Nonfiction: 6" x 9"
- Memoir: 5.25" x 8"

Other popular sizes suggested online include:

- Romance: 5.25" x 8"
- Trade Paperbacks: 5" x 8" to 6" x 9"
- Hardcover books (most commonly) 6" x 9."

PAGE COUNT

Average lengths:

- Flash Fiction: Under 1,500 words
- Short Story: 1,500–7,500 words
- Novelette: 7,500–17,500 words
- Novella: 17,500–40,000 words
- Novel: 40,000 words plus
- Middle Grade: 20,000–40,000 words
- Young Adult: 50,000–80,000 words
- Historical: 80,000–100,000 words
- Mystery/Thriller: 70,000–90,000 words
- Romance: 40,000–100,000 words
- Science Fiction: 90,000–110,000 words
- Self-Help: 40,000–50,000 words
- Memoir: 80,000–100,000 words
- Biography: 80,000 words plus

PAPER COLOR & WEIGHT

Fifty-pound non-glossy paper in white or cream is commonly used for books that are mainly text (novels). However, a few years ago, I published a book with color illustrations, and I found that 70lb. paper works better with illustrations.

If you publish a "coffee table" book with high-quality photographs, you may want to ask for coated paper, which is more expensive but richer looking.

The heavier the paper, the higher the cost. The more pages, the higher the cost. Keep this in mind while writing your masterpiece. If your book costs a small fortune to print, and you have to charge a higher price than the market will bear, you may have fewer sales. And if the book is too heavy to hold, people may give up before they finish reading it. If you've already edited out all the unnecessary scenes and your book is still lengthy, consider dividing it into parts and releasing the parts a few months apart. However, that would mean additional covers (perhaps different colors of the same design) plus adding *Part One* or *Part Two,* etc., under the title. You would also need a different back cover summary, ISBN, and bar code for each book. The benefit is you could tease the upcoming book in the back of the current book.

BINDING

Page count and cover type will usually dictate bookbinding styles:

- Case Binding: hardcover binding. The cover is slightly larger than the pages inside.

- Perfect Binding: paperback binding. The cover is the same size as the pages, which are glued to the spine. The minimum number of pages required for a perfect binding varies depending on the printing company you use. Some ask for a 30-page minimum, while IngramSpark requires 45. Another company I saw online wanted no less than 60 pages for a perfect-bound book.

- Saddle Stitch: magazines or manuals less than 30 pages are usually stapled through the fold line. They used to be sewn together, hence the name *saddle stitch*.

- Spiral Coil Binding: workbooks, planners, etc. A continuous spiral is threaded through holes, allowing books to open flat.

BARCODE

Print books need barcodes. Bowker sells barcodes; however, if you search online, you can find sites allowing you to convert your ISBN to a barcode for free. If you don't trust downloading a barcode from an unknown site, Bowker charges $25.00 for one. Bowkerbarcode.com gives a slightly reduced rate when multiples are purchased.

Barcode Pricing

1-5	$25 per barcode
6-10	$23 per barcode
11+	$21 per barcode

BACK-COVER SUMMARY

The cover of your book will capture a potential reader's attention, but the back cover or dust jacket summary—also known as a blurb—will sell it. The whole purpose of the blurb is to intrigue readers and appeal to their emotions.

A book blurb is not a synopsis of your novel. You don't want to give everything away. You just want to pique readers' interest. Do it with short, precise sentences. Limit yourself to 150 words. And if you know anything about SEO, this is the place to use keywords.

LOGLINE

A logline is a single sentence that summarizes the central conflict of your plot in a way that hooks the reader. The term originated in old Hollywood, where studios kept logbooks with a one-line description of every film they made.

Examples:

Titanic – "A seventeen-year-old aristocrat falls in love with a kind but poor artist aboard the luxurious, ill-fated R.M.S. Titanic."

Back to the Future: "A young man is transported to the past, where he must reunite his parents before he and his future cease to exist."

Se7en: "Two homicide detectives are on a desperate hunt for a serial killer whose crimes are based on the seven deadly sins."

ELEVATOR PITCH

An elevator pitch is usually one or two sentences that summarize your book in a way that hooks a potential agent or publisher. Its name comes from the time it takes to travel between floors in an elevator when you suddenly find yourself face-to-face with an agent you want to pitch to. Your pitch should be short and snappy—and preferably less than twenty-five words. If they want to hear more, they'll ask you.

BOOK PRICE

When you price your print books, The price needs to be high enough to cover the cost of printing, shipping, and handling yet low enough to entice potential readers who have never heard of you. You don't have the same concerns with e-books because there are no printing costs. However, you still want to make the price high enough to help you earn back the expenses of editing the book, having a cover professionally designed, paying for the ISBN, registering copyright if you choose to do so, and all the other various costs of writing, publishing, and marketing your book (author website hosting, online courses, writing conferences, etc.). You won't make it all back by selling one book. However, over time, selling a large number of books could help you recoup your costs.

Writing is something you can do practically for free. All you need is a pen and paper. It's turning your words into a published book that takes money.

ROYALTIES

The sales price of your book will determine your royalties. The outlets you choose to sell it will decide the percentage you'll receive for each sale.

Hardcover and paperback book royalties are on the lower end of the scale (anywhere between 5 percent and 15 percent).

E-books, pay a better royalty rate, which could be as high as 70 percent in some cases. Amazon allows authors to have a little more say in their e-book royalty rate, so the following section is specifically about Amazon.

The lowest amount Amazon will allow you to charge for a book is ninety-nine cents for an e-book up to three megabytes, which is a relatively short book. Your royalty would be 35 percent minus any applicable taxes at that price point.

On public domain e-book sales, regardless of the length of the work, Amazon only pays a 35 percent royalty based on the list price minus any applicable taxes.

For books priced between $2.99 and $9.99, you can elect to be paid a 70 percent royalty by Amazon. That amount is based on the sale price minus applicable taxes minus delivery costs.

You will need to select the 70% option when setting your price in that range on KDP.

Pricing, royalty, and distribution	Select a royalty plan and set your Kindle eBook list prices below ○ 35% ◉ 70%

To be eligible for a 70 percent e-book royalty, you must also have a "physical" (print, audio, etc.) version of your book, and Amazon says the matching e-book must be priced at least 20 percent lower than the print edition.

On books priced higher than $9.99, Amazon only pays a 35 percent royalty.

It is possible to sell a book for less than $2.99 on Amazon, but only if you can prove you are selling it for less on other venues. Then, Amazon will usually match the price.

Amazon does not always sell your book for the price you listed it at. The company is known to lower the price of a book if there is any indication that sales will increase at a lower cost. Their sales price will affect the amount of your royalty.

INDIE AUTHORS USER'S GUIDE

ADVERTISING & MARKETING

ADVERTISING & MARKETING

Whether you prefer business cards, promotional items like pens with your book's name on them, or paid advertising on sites like BookBub, Bargain Booksy, and the Fussy Librarian, the more you do to promote yourself and your book, the better. However, some promotions can be costly and return little profit. Shop around.

I have a permafree book that I pay to advertise, yet I receive no royalties in return. I occasionally pay for advertising because there is usually an uptick in the sale of subsequent books in the series. Plus, it helps my Amazon ranking when buyers upload a few hundred books in one day. Do I do this every month? No. But I do it three or four times a year for the series to capture new readers.

Several book sites put out daily listings of e-books that are on sale or free. Experiment carefully to determine which ones work best for you.

WEBSITE

Every writer should have a website. It's a place to showcase your books with links to sales venues while also including content so readers can learn more about you. And if you spend some time creating blogs, podcasts, or videos, you can showcase them on your website.

BLOGS, PODCASTS & VIDEOS

Some of the best ways to promote your book are with blogs, podcasts, and videos. You can give people writing advice or talk about where your story ideas come from. You can relate funny anecdotes about your writing process or provide extra insight into characters.

Your method can be as simple as writing a couple of hundred words about how you set the mood for your scenes, or holding your phone at arm's length for a minute or two while talking about your prewriting ritual.

Some of you may prefer setting up a ring light, investing in a microphone, and adding graphics and production value to regular video episodes about your writer's journey for YouTube. Do whatever suits you best. Engaging with the public is a terrific way to promote your work.

KEYWORDS

Keywords help make books more discoverable. They are the words that readers type into a search engine to find their perfect book. For example, a parent might type in the keywords "juvenile fantasy" to find a book for their child. Or they may be more specific and type in words like "princess" or "unicorns."

Keywords, or multi-word keyword strings, describe the content of your book. If you're writing a romance novel that takes place in 1815, you might use the keyword *Regency romance*. Or perhaps you want to draw attention to your protagonist with the keyword string *strong female lead*.

If your story is more about the setting, your keyword might be *Wild West* or *post-apocalyptic New York*. You could call attention to the theme of your story with keywords like *coming of age* or *young love*. The more keywords—often used as popular descriptors—that you can incorporate into your website (or any web description of your book), the more it will help drive traffic to your site.

Choose keywords that best describe your book, and incorporate them into your title, back cover summary, and metadata.

SEO

Search engine optimization uses strategies like keywords and backlinks to increase your website's visibility and to allow search engines to find it.

Use keywords in your metadata and include your title, book summary, and logline. Build alliances with other authors and influencers and ask to build links to each other's websites. The whole idea behind SEO is to make it easier for people to find you.

BACKLINKS

A backlink is a hyperlink from one web page to another. You can link your readers to sites that support something you discuss in your book or your website. However, you also want to have those sites' authors or organizations link back to you. Backlinks give your website credibility.

SOCIAL MEDIA

Social media is both a blessing and a curse. It can boost your visibility as an author and your book's popularity. However, it can also drag you into a black hole of lost productivity, where you become so interested in seeing what everyone else is doing that you forego working on your manuscript.

In the beginning, limit yourself to one or two social media sites. You can always add to that once you launch your book and have additional time. But don't get too caught up in it because you need to start writing your next book. Nothing will help your career as an author like adding more novels to your list. Think of it as strength in numbers.

PRINTERS & SELF-PUBLISHING SITES

There are several places where you can print copies of your book on demand, which allows authors and vendors to order only as many books as they want. Your choice of printer/distributor may depend on your goals for your book.

Some printer/distributors charge a fee to set up your book and cover. Others provide services like marketing or design for an additional price. And some may encourage you to buy a package deal.

Below, I've listed four printer/distributors that I have personally used in the past. This list is not an *endorsement* of any one of these companies—just a starting point for you. Do your due diligence. That means getting on the Internet and looking up each company that you're considering. See what they have to offer and how much they charge. See what other similar companies are listed that you might be interested in. You're the publisher. It's your call.

AMAZON – e-book, paperback, hardcover
https://kdp.amazon.com/en_US/help/topic/G200620010

INGRAMSPARK – e-book, paperback, hardcover
https://www.ingramspark.com

LULU – paperback, hardcover
https://www.lulu.com

DRAFT2DIGITAL – e-book, paperback
https://www.draft2digital.com

CONCLUSION

This guide is by no means comprehensive. Consider it a jumping-off point on the road to self-publishing your novel. I have tried to include all the information that I repeatedly looked up when I first started out. I hope the guidance I have shared here speeds you on your journey to publication.

RESOURCES

Amazon
Draft2Digital
IngramSpark
Jericho Writers
Lulu
MasterClass
ProWritingAid
Wikipedia
Writers.com

AUTHOR BIO

Carol Pack is an award-winning former journalist who gave up fact for fiction. After discussing her vision of the perfect library, she was inspired to write the Library of Illumination series (under the pen name C. A. Pack). The book that gave birth to the series *Chronicles: The Library of Illumination* received a starred review from Kirkus Reviews, which named it one of the "Best Indie Books of 2014."

In addition, she is the co-author (under the name Carol Pack) of several non-fiction, self-help books, including *Over-Sixty: Shades of Gray*. She also co-authored its companion puzzle/coloring book, *Mind Games & Soporifics*, an all-too-real look at the COVID-19 pandemic in *Our Coronavirus Diary*, and *The Book of Lists*.

After years of copyediting reporters' stories, creating and writing content for three websites, and writing and publishing more than twenty fiction and nonfiction books, Carol became certified as a *proofreader* and *copy editor* and now uses her experience to help indie authors polish their manuscripts.

Now, with the addition of the *Indie Author User's Guide,* she hopes to help them publish their work as well.

You can learn more about the author on her website:

https://www.carolpack.com

www.ingramcontent.com/pod-product-compliance
Lightning Source LLC
Chambersburg PA
CBHW071217120626
46546CB00006B/2603